TORNADOES!
New and Updated

BY GAIL GIBBONS

Holiday House • New York

In memory of Coleen Salley

Special thanks to Eric Evenson of
the National Weather Service,
South Burlington, Vermont.

Special thanks to Dave Jones, founder,
president, and CEO of StormCenter
Communications, Inc., Ellicott City,
Maryland.

Special thanks to Chris Vaccaro
of the National Oceanic and
Atmospheric Administration.

Printed in July 2018 at Tien Wah Press,
Johor Bahru, Johor, Malaysia.
www.holidayhouse.com
Second Edition
1 3 5 7 9 10 8 6 4 2
The Library of Congress has catalogued the prior
edition as follows:
Gibbons, Gail.
Tornadoes! / by Gail Gibbons.—1st ed.
p. cm.
ISBN: 978-0-8234-2216-6 (hardcover)
ISBN: 978-0-8234-4187-7 (paperback)
1. Tornadoes—Juvenile literature. I. Title.
QC955.2.G53 2009
551.55'3—dc22
2008035828

The word TORNADO comes from the Spanish word *tronada*, meaning "thunderstorm."

It is raining hard; the winds are strong. The sky is dark. Suddenly a twisting column of moist air reaches down from a cloud and touches the ground. It makes a loud, roaring sound. It is a tornado!

3

LIGHTNING

CUMULONIMBUS CLOUDS

RAIN

HAIL is frozen rain in the form of ice pellets, which may be the size of golf balls or even larger.

Tornadoes begin inside storm clouds called cumulonimbus (KYOOM-yoo-low-NIM-bus) clouds, which are made up of warm, moist air. These large, dark clouds can grow to be tall and enormous. There is lightning, thunder, rain, hail, and high winds.

A THUNDERHEAD is a very large, dark cumulonimbus cloud or group of cumulonimbus clouds.

CONDENSATION occurs when moist, warm air cools and turns into a liquid such as rain.

UPDRAFT

DOWNDRAFT

HEAT ALWAYS RISES

When warm, humid air rises from the ground toward a dark cumulonimbus thunderhead, it creates an updraft that pulls more warm, humid air with it. When the air rises to where the temperature is cooler, condensation occurs, creating rain or hail. The cool air falls back toward Earth, creating a downdraft.

If the updraft and the downdraft come together and start to spin, a funnel-shaped cloud forms inside the thunderhead and sometimes tilts into a funnel that reaches down toward the ground.

Tornadoes may occur at any time of the year if the weather conditions are right.

As the funnel cloud spins faster and faster, it sucks up more and more warm air and becomes bigger and louder and more powerful. If it touches the ground, a tornado is born.

The letter *F* represents *Fujita.*

The letter *E* represents *Enhanced.*

EF-0

EF-5

In 1971, T. Theodore Fujita developed the Fujita Tornado Scale, rating tornadoes on a scale from F0 to F5. Since then, the scale has been enhanced, setting stricter standards for measuring damage. Since 2007, the Enhanced Fujita Tornado Scale has been used to classify tornadoes from EF-0 to EF-5.

Classifications are mostly based on the amount and type of damage caused. There is no way yet to directly measure the winds in every tornado. Wind speeds are estimates only and are based on the severity of the damage. No matter how big or little a tornado is or how long it lasts on the ground, it is likely to cause damage.

ENHANCED FUJITA TORNADO SCALE

EF-0 TORNADOES

EF-0 tornadoes may have wind speeds between 65 mph (104.6 kph) and 85 mph (136.8 kph).

mph = miles per hour
kph = kilometers per hour

They can damage chimneys, break limbs off trees, and blow over shallow-rooted trees.

EF-1 TORNADOES

EF-1 tornadoes may have wind speeds between 86 mph (138.4 kph) and 110 mph (177 kph).

They can peel the surface off roofs and overturn small trucks and mobile homes.

EF-2 TORNADOES

EF-2 tornadoes may have wind speeds between 111 mph (178.6 kph) and 135 mph (216 kph).

They can tear the whole roof off a frame house, demolish mobile homes, and snap or uproot large trees.

EF-3 TORNADOES

EF-3 tornadoes may have wind speeds between 136 mph (218.9 kph) and 165 mph (265.5 kph).

They can uproot a forest and lift heavy cars off the ground.

EF-4 TORNADOES

EF-4 tornadoes may have wind speeds between 166 mph (267.2 kph) and 200 mph (321.9 kph).

They can demolish well-constructed houses, leaving few walls standing. Other structures may be blown off their foundations and moved some distance.

EF-5 TORNADOES

EF-5 tornadoes are the most violent tornadoes. They have wind speeds of more than 200 mph (321.9 kph).

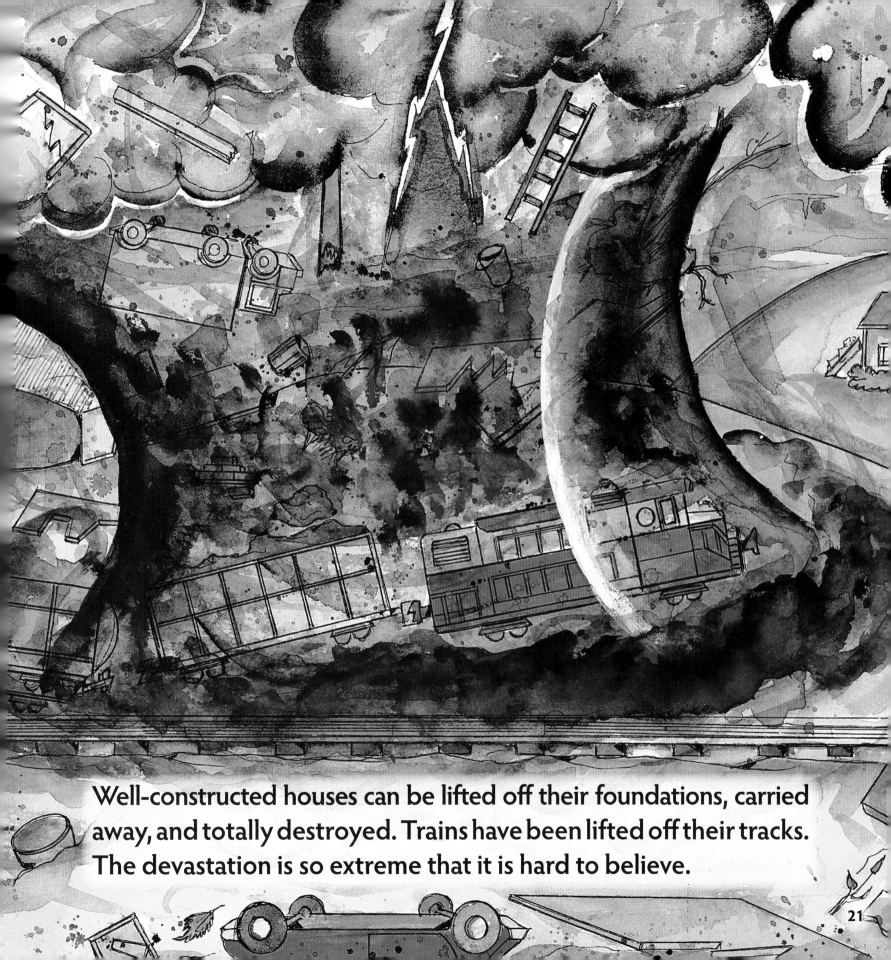

Well-constructed houses can be lifted off their foundations, carried away, and totally destroyed. Trains have been lifted off their tracks. The devastation is so extreme that it is hard to believe.

TORNADO ALLEY

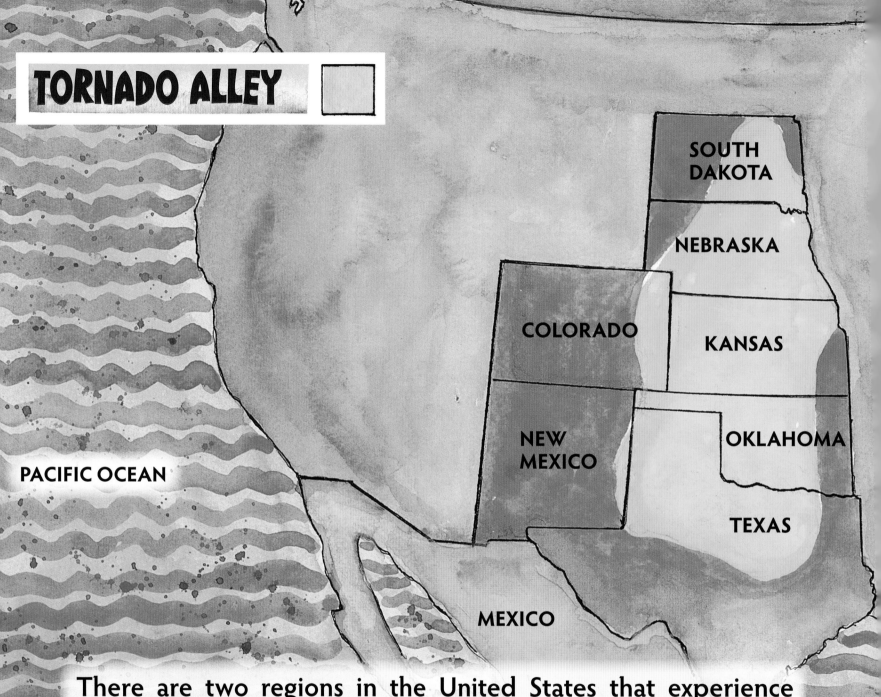

There are two regions in the United States that experience tornadoes frequently. One region is in the middle section of the country, where most of the violent tornadoes occur. It is often referred to as Tornado Alley. In this area most tornadoes occur during April, May, and June.

CANADA

UNITED STATES

ATLANTIC OCEAN

FLORIDA

The other is the state of Florida, where most tornadoes occur during January, February, and March. The United States has about 1,200 tornadoes a year, more than any other country.

On May 3, 1999, ninety-six tornadoes ravaged parts of Texas, Oklahoma, Kansas, Nebraska, and South Dakota. If the EF scale had been in effect when the tornadoes occurred, the most destructive ones would have been classified EF-5.

The damage in the Oklahoma City area alone was valued at more than one billion dollars.

On the afternoon of March 18, 1925, a record-breaking tornado devastated parts of Missouri, Illinois, and Indiana. It is called the Great Tri-State Tornado.

An estimated 695 people died. It is believed 606 people died in Illinois alone. The tornado was on the ground for 3 hours and 29 minutes and traveled 217 miles (349.2 km). If the EF scale had been in effect at this time, this tornado also may have been classified EF-5.

METEOROLOGISTS are scientists who study weather.

Meteorologists are on constant watch to predict and warn people of dangerous storms that may produce tornadoes. They study computer data and radar screens.

The National Weather Service will issue a Tornado Watch when tornadoes are possible. They will issue a Tornado Warning for a specific area when a tornado is likely to form or has been spotted. This information is immediately broadcast on television, radio, the Internet, and mobile phones.

WHAT TO DO WHEN A TORNADO APPROACHES

If your house has a basement, go to it at once.

If you are in a house without a basement, go to an interior closet or bathroom far from the outside walls.

Crouch down low and cover your head with your hands. Stay away from windows and outside walls.

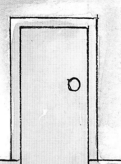

Try to cover yourself with a mattress or heavy blankets for protection from falling debris.

If you can,
crouch under
a set of stairs.

If you are in a car, get out immediately! Try to find a low spot, such as a ditch, to lie in. Lie flat on your stomach and cover your head with your hands.

After the tornado, be careful of fallen electrical wires, broken glass, and unsafe structures.

Try to have an adult help you!

TORNADO HAPPENINGS...

Most tornadoes occur in the afternoon.

Most tornadoes last less than 10 minutes.

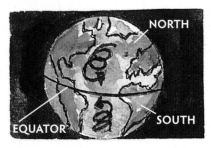

Most tornadoes rotate counterclockwise in the Northern Hemisphere (north of the equator) and clockwise in the Southern Hemisphere (south of the equator).

In the United States, only the National Weather Service issues tornado watches and warnings nationwide.

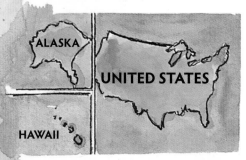

Tornadoes have occurred in all fifty states of the USA.

Funnel clouds form over water too. When they touch down on water, they are called waterspouts.

Most tornadoes are classified EF-0 or EF-1. EF-5 tornadoes are very rare. On May 22, 2011, an EF-5 tornado struck Joplin, Missouri, and caused catastrophic damage.

WEBSITES

In the United States:
http://www.spc.noaa.gov/faq/tornado/

In Canada:
http://www.ec.gc.ca/

English: search *tornado*

Français: recherche *tornade*